AIRTAG
USER GUIDE

A Complete Step By Step Guide On How To Get The Most Use Of Your Airtag, With The Aid Of Pictures, Tips And Shortcuts

BY

PETER J. SCOTT

D1234814

DISCLAIMER:

The information contained in this book is for educational purposes only. All efforts have been executed to present accurate, reliable, and up-to-date information contained herein. By reading this document, the reader agrees that under no circumstances is the author responsible for any losses, direct or indirect, which are incurred as a result of the information contained in this book including errors, omissions, and inaccuracy.

Table of Contents

INTRODUCTION

Apple today introduced AirTag, a small, elegantly designed accessory that helps you track and find the products that work best with Apple Find My. Whether attached to a handbag, keys, backpack, or other items, AirTag takes advantage of the vast, global Find My1 network to help you find lost items, all while maintaining private and anonymous location data. The AirTag is available in single and four packs for just $ 29 and $ 99, respectively, and will be available from Friday, April 30th.

I am excited to this incredible new capability to iPhone users with the introduction of AirTag, leveraging the vast Find My network to help them track and find the important items in their lives, With its design, unparalleled recognition experience, an integrated privacy, and security features, AirTag offers customers additional tools to harness the power of Apple's ecosystem and enhance the versatility of the iPhone."

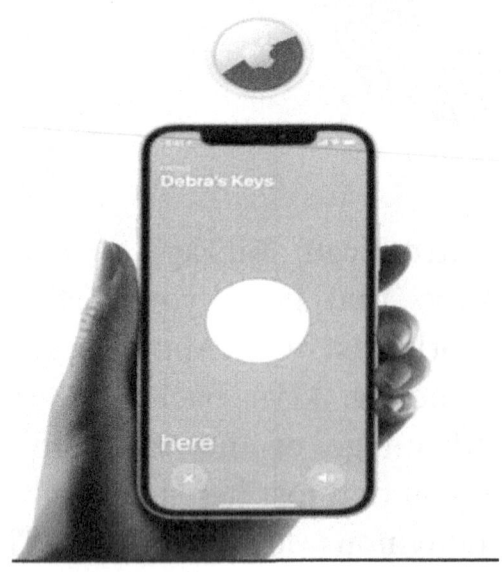

iPhone 12, which displays a screen that detects the AirTag and the AirTag device.

LIGHTWEIGHT DESIGN WITH MAGICAL SETTINGS

All-round AirTags are small and lightweight, precision engraved, brushed stainless steel, and IP67 resistant to water and dust. 2 Built-in speaker makes it easy to find the AirTag, while removable cover makes it easy to change users The AirTag has the same magical setup experience as the AirPods - just bring the AirTag closer to iPhone and you'll connect. Users can assign an AirTag to an item and name it by default, such as "Keys" or "Jacket," or enter a custom name of their choice.

iPhone 12 displays the AirTag setup screen, along with the AirTag.

The simple setup magically connects AirTag to your iPhone, iPad, or iPod touch.

Customers can customize the AirTag for free engraving, including text and a selection of 31 emoticons, when they purchase from Apple.com or the Apple Store app.

Users can easily put the AirTag themselves in a bag or pocket, or use a wide range of Apple-designed AirTag accessories, including a lightweight and durable polyurethane loop and a leather loop and leather keychain 4. Contains specially tanned European leather. The closure of each accessory fits snugly to the AirTag while securely securing the user's belongings, further customizing the AirTag while ensuring it is always with your important items.

The AirTag can be placed stand-alone in a bag or pocket or used with a wide range of Apple-designed AirTag accessories with free, personalized engraving, including text and emoji selection.

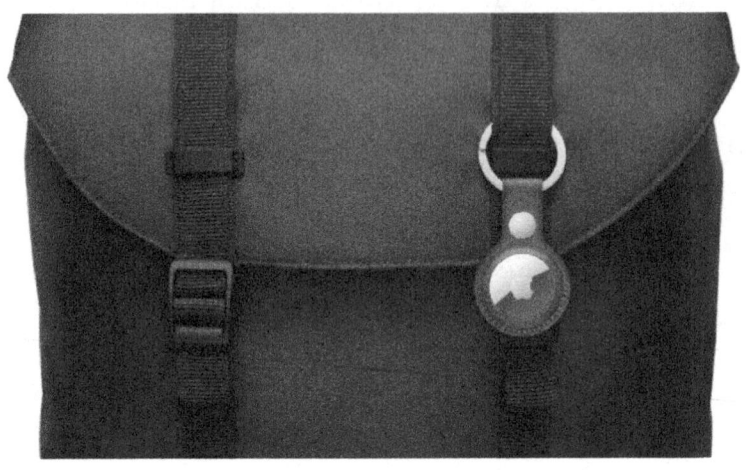

AirTag with a leather keychain, attached to a messager bag.

COMPREHENSIVE SEARCH EXPERIENCE

After setting up AirTag, it appears on the New Items tab in Find My, where users can see the current or last known location of the item on the map.

If a user places their battery incorrectly and is within Bluetooth range, they can use the Find My app to play AirTag audio to help them find it. Users can also ask Siri to locate your item and AirTag will sound when it is nearby.

Many items with AirTag are listed on the Items tab of the Find My app on iPhone 12.

Users can track AirTag on the New Items tab in the Find My app.

Each AirTag is equipped with Apple's U1 chips using ultra-wideband technology, which allows Precision Search5 for iPhone 11 and iPhone 12 users. This advanced technology more accurately determines the distance and direction of a lost AirTag when it is within range. As the user moves, Precision Detection reads the fuses from the camera, ARKit, accelerometer, and gyroscope and then leads them to the AirTag with a combination of sound, haptics, and visual feedback.

Precision sensing with AirTag provides fuses from the camera, ARKit, accelerometer, and gyroscope to an iPhone to provide a more accurate, directional detection experience.

If your AirTag is separate from its owner and not within range of Bluetooth, the Find My network can help you keep track of it. The My Find network is approaching a billion Apple devices and notices lost Bluetooth signals from the AirTag and can share the space back to its owner, all in the background, anonymously and privately.

Users can also put the AirTag in lost mode and be notified when it is within range or when it is found by the vast Find My network. If someone finds the lost AirTag, it can be exploited on their iPhone or any NFC-enabled device and taken to a website that will show the owner a contact phone number if made available.

AirTag supports support for iOS's built-in accessibility features. For example, searching for accuracy using VoiceOver can direct blind or partially sighted users to AirTag, with instructions for "AirTag is 9 meters to the left."

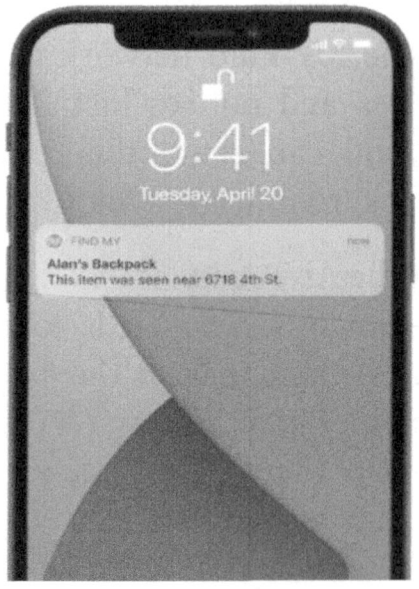

If the AirTag disappears, the Find My network can help track it and send a notification to the user when it is found.

PRIVACY AND SECURITY

AirTag has been designed from the ground up to keep location data secret and secure. AirTag does not keep location data or history on its servers. Communication with the Find My network is encrypted between endpoints, so only the device owner has access to their location data, and no one, including Apple, knows the identity or location of the device that helped them find it.

The AirTag is also designed with proactive features that deter unwanted tracking, especially for the industry. AirTag's Bluetooth signal IDs frequently rotate to prevent unauthorized location tracking. IOS devices can also detect an AirTag that is not owned by the owner and notify the user if an unknown AirTag appears to be traveling with them from one place to another over time. And even if users don't have an iOS device, an AirTag that is separate from its owner will sound for a longer period when they move to draw attention to it.

If a user discovers an unknown AirTag, they can take advantage of it with their iPhone or NFC-enabled device, and the instructions provide instructions for disconnecting the unknown AirTag.

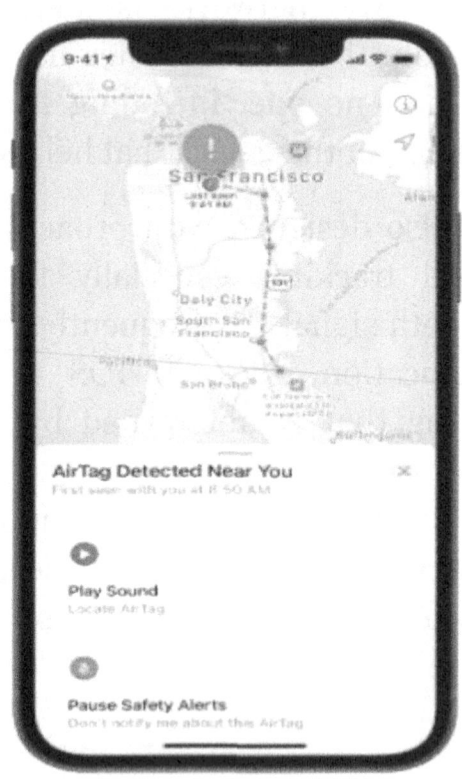

IOS devices can detect an unattended AirTag and notify the user if an unknown AirTag appears to be traveling with them over time.

AIRTAG AND HERMÈS

Apple and Hermès introduce the Hermès AirTag, an elegant blend of handmade leather accessories including a magic bag, keychain, travel tag, and luggage tag. Hermès accessories are sold together with a specially engraved AirTag based on the brand's iconic Clou de Selle's signature.

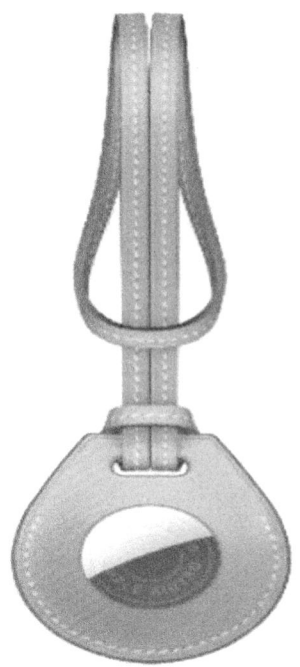

The AirTag Hermès features an elegant blend of handmade leather accessories, including a magic bag, keychain, travel tag, and luggage tag - all sold together with a specially engraved AirTag based on the brand's iconic Clou de Selle's signature.

THE FIND MY NETWORK ACCESSORY PROGRAM

Third-party products and accessories may also increase the support available with the new Find My network add-on. Through the program, device and product manufacturers can now integrate detection capabilities directly into their products, using the Advanced Find My network, incorporating uncompromising privacy, allowing customers to find other important elements of their lives using Find My.

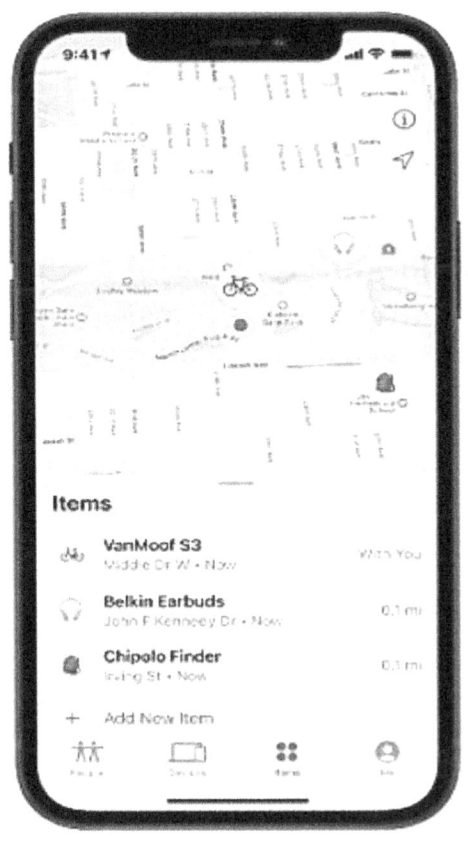

With the Find My Network Network Accessory, the powerful and secure Find My network now helps users find and keep track of even the most important items in their lives using the Items tab in the My My app.

COMMITTED TO THE ENVIRONMENT

Today, Apple is carbon-neutral in terms of global corporate operations, and by 2030, it plans to have the net impact of air conditioning across the entire business, including manufacturing supply chains and supply cycles, throughout the product's life. This means that all Apple devices sold, from the material collection, parts manufacturing, assembly, shipping, customer use, charging, all the way to recycling and material recovery, will be 100% carbon neutral. . AirTag will use 100% recycled tin to solder the main logic board, is free of harmful substances and is very energy efficient, and will use wood in packaging from recycled or responsibly managed forests.

PRICES AND AVAILABILITY

- ➢ Customers can order an AirTag from 5 a.m. PDT on Friday, April 23rd.

- The AirTag will be available in one and four-packs for $ 29 (US) and $ 99 (US) through Apple.com, the Apple Store app, Apple Store locations, and Apple Authorized Resellers and selected carriers (prices are subject to change) April It starts on Friday, the 30th.
- Apple-designed AirTag accessories include a leather keychain in saddle brown, (PRODUCT) RED and Baltic Blue for $ 35 (US); saddle brown leather loop and (PRODUCT) RED for $ 39 (US); and white, deep navy, sunflower, and electric orange polyurethane rings for $ 29 (US).
- The AirTag Hermès includes the premium magic bag and keychain in Fauve Barenia leather, Bleu Indigo and orange, and the Baggage Tag and Travel Tag6 labels in Fauve Barenia leather, all available from Friday, April 30th.
- Shop on apple.com or the Apple Store and add a free, personalized slice.

CHAPTER ONE

FEATURES

- Find application tracking
- Precision search
- Ask Siri to find out
- Smooth setting

Apple AirTag is designed to keep track of everyday objects such as keys or a backpack. It integrates seamlessly with iOS with access and control via the Find My app on your Apple device.

DESIGN

- 32mm diameter, 6mm thickness (TBC)
- IP67 protection
- User removable CR2032 battery
- Customization available

Apple AirTag is a circular device. It has a laser-polished stainless steel surface that gives it a slightly premium look than some of its competitors, while also being distinguished by its circular shape.

The AirTag has a user-removable battery - which is said to last about a year. This is a standard CR2032 cell that is so easy to buy when it needs to be replaced.

It has a built-in speaker, water, and dust-resistant IP67, which allows the measuring pit to be used in water for 30 minutes.

Apple AirTag can also be customized, such as with emoticons or names. There are also several accessories available for the AirTag, including keychains and lines that allow the AirTag to be easily attached to various objects such as backpacks.

PRECISION FINDING

Apple AirTags are small button-shaped devices designed to attach to items such as keys and wallets that allow you to track these accessories via Bluetooth with just one app on your Apple device.

If you set up AirTag and attach it to an item, you can track the item mentioned in the Find My app when it runs out.

I use the lost AirTag's Bluetooth signals to distribute its location to its owner. However, in addition to Bluetooth, each AirTag includes an Ultra-Wideband U1 chip, and a device that also includes U1 chips has a Precision Detection feature that allows you to determine distance and direction more accurately, when It's in range, compared to Bluetooth only.

If you're looking to find a lost object and have an iPhone 11 or 12, Precision Detection directs you to the exact location of the lost AirTag using the camera, accelerometer, and gyroscope, voice, haptics, and visual feedback. It should be used here.

HOW TO FIND THE EXACT AIRTAG LOCATION

1. On your iPhone, open the Find My app.
2. Tap Items.
3. Tap the AirTag whose exact location you want to get.

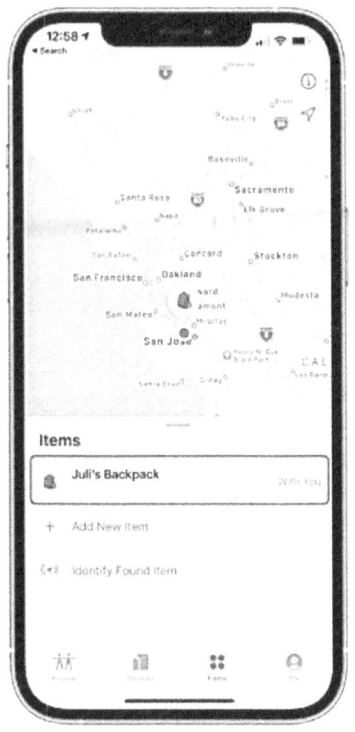 

4. Tap Destination. It should be labeled "Close" below if the Precision Detection function is available.

5. Now start moving to find the AirTag and follow the on-screen instructions. You should see an open one pointing in the direction of the AirTag, an approximate distance that tells you how far it is, and a note if you're on another floor.

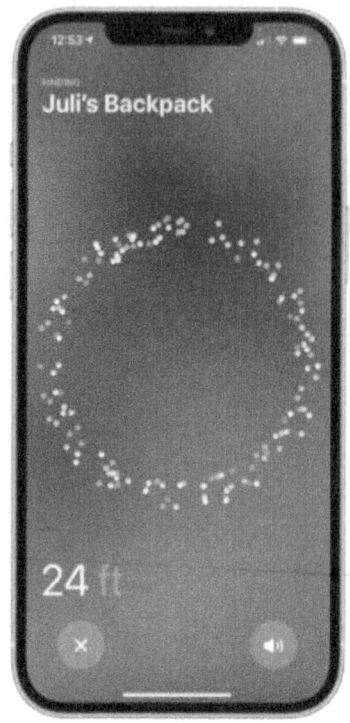

When you approach an object, you will feel a tactical response on your phone, and beeps will indicate that you are approaching an object. The graphics on the iPhone AirTag will also change as you get closer to it. Search Precision appears when you have successfully found your AirTag and your iPhone or Apple device is very close.

Keep in mind that ultra-wideband is not supported worldwide, so Precision Detection does not work in some countries. For more details, read our guide on what you need to know when traveling abroad with AirTags.

ENGRAVING AIRTAGS

AirTag Allows only 6 characters and 5 engraving emoticons or emoticons, text, or numbers. See the examples below.

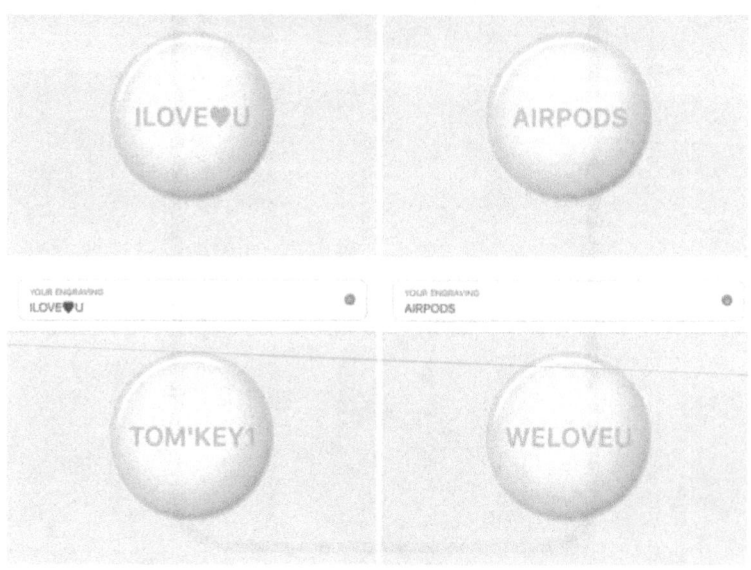

Airtag-engraving-characters-limit up to 6 characters and 5 emoji characters

- ➢ If you add more than 6 characters or 5 emoticons, select red: "Message does not fit in the available space".
- ➢ [Apple keyboard emoji is not supported, otherwise, you will receive the error message "These characters cannot be engraved"]

Add emoji with one click. Enter text or numbers.

You can even mix multiple emoticons with text.

Engraving-keyboard

WHAT TO ENGRAVE INTO THE ENTIRE NEW APPLE AIRTAG.

➤ Poop Emoji engraving is one of the hottest favorite emojis in our American culture.

➤ MY- one of the funny Airtag engravings

- ➤ Single Emoticon - If you want to see a great emoticon on an airplane label, just add one emoticon that is your favorite.
- ➤ You can add your date of birth and month number to the numbers.

or you can enter your year of birth.

- ➤ Couple Emoji - Add one emoticon to your favorite and another to your loved one.

HERE ARE SOME EXAMPLES OF INTERESTING, FUNNY, COOL, AND BETTER CUSTOMIZATION

1. MOM
2. LOVE (EMOJI) - LOVE ♥
3. MY CAT (EMOJI) – CAT
4. HKEY - For House key
5. OKEY – For Office key
6. BKEY - For Bike key
7. CKEY – For Car key
8. MYKEY

9. The name of the Kitten
10.   DOG (EMOJI) – DOG
11. Your Dog NAME
12. LO (EMOJI) L
13. LOVE (Emoji) Name your first character or anything you crave the most
14. Year of birth - 1990

A lucky number with up to four digits

15. Nickname

CHAPTER TWO

AIRTAG BATTERY

Here's how to replace the battery in your AirTag and how you will know when to change it.

The AirTag battery will last for about a year, and your iPhone will alert you when the battery is low. But if you just rely on this notification, you can see that there may be problems.

For example, the battery warning may run low in the first hour of a two-week cruise. And the lost luggage gets out of the boat at the end of the voyage.

You can be sure that Apple won't wait until the last minute to get a low-battery notification. However, the reason Apple can only roughly estimate that an AirTag battery lasts a year depends on usage.

And you use it when you have lost something. So here's a suggestion on how to maximize battery life in your AirTag before you need to replace it.

HOW TO MAXIMIZE AIRTAG BATTERY LIFE

1. Do not activate the AirTag until you need it.
2. Once activated, place "Replace AirTag Battery" in the To-Do application
3. Set this task to repeat every 11 months
4. Add a tag like "vacation"

There will be AirTags that you activated the moment you entered them, such as the ones you put on your keychain. But those you take with you to your luggage can wait until they leave.

The To-Do app encourages you to at least be careful about notifying Apple of a low battery level. But if this app also allows you to tag or mark tasks, before you go on a trip, you can get to show all the "To Dos" marked with "vacation".

So anytime you're traveling, you'll see "Replace your AirTag battery" and you can make an informed decision about whether it's close to 12 months or not.

However, whether you do it early, wait for the notification, or after the battery is completely discharged, you will need to replace it sometime.

REPLACING THE BATTERY IN AN AIRTAG

1. Rotate the AirTag with the silver side facing up
2. Press the opposite ends of the silver coating with your thumb
3. Keep pressing and turn left
4. If the silver top is loose, remove it
5. Remove the battery that is now exposed
6. Insert a new CR2032 battery with a positive + sign
7. Replace the silver top cover
8. Press down with your thumb and turn the cover to the right

You hear the AirTag make a little sound, very similar to what you hear if you ever need to reset it. And then you're done.

RANGE OF AIRTAG

Apple hasn't officially released the exact range of AirTags, but since they connect to iPhones and even Android phones via Bluetooth, we can say the range is about 30 feet or ten meters for those who use the system.

If your items exceed a range of 30 meters, AirTags will start making noise.

The range may vary depending on the current conditions. In some areas, you can identify the AirTag beyond 30 meters. When this happens, the area will usually be very open and there will not be many obstacles to interfering with the signal.

Other times you will find that you can barely notice it, even if it is only 20 meters away. Walls and large objects can interfere with the Bluetooth or NFC signal, so the answer is not perfect.

According to other sources, because Bluetooth 5.0 has a range of 800 feet or 240 meters, you can follow AirTag in this range. However, we still have to wait for this because no one has tested it yet.

CHAPTER THREE

RETURNING LOST AIRTAG

Apple AirTag battery trackers are designed to allow users to keep track of their daily possessions, such as keys, wallets, sports, and more. If you find an AirTag that has been separated from its owner, you can safely restore it as follows.

AirTags may be monitored using Apple's Find My app, which searches for them using Bluetooth and other Apple devices.

However, if the AirTag is not nearby and there are no Apple devices in the area, "Find My" can only tell the owner where he was last on the map.

In such cases, the AirTag owner can put it in lost mode, allowing anyone with an NFC-compatible iPhone or Android device to help return the AirTag. Even if the AirTag is not in lost mode, if it is separated from its owner for a while, it will sound an alert to alert those nearby.

If you come across an AirTag and have an NFC-enabled device, you can do the following to get it back to its rightful owner.

1. Touch and hold the top of your iPhone or NFC-enabled smartphone on the white side of the AirTag.
2. Tap the notification on the device screen. This takes you to a webpage where you may learn more about the AirTag, including its serial number.

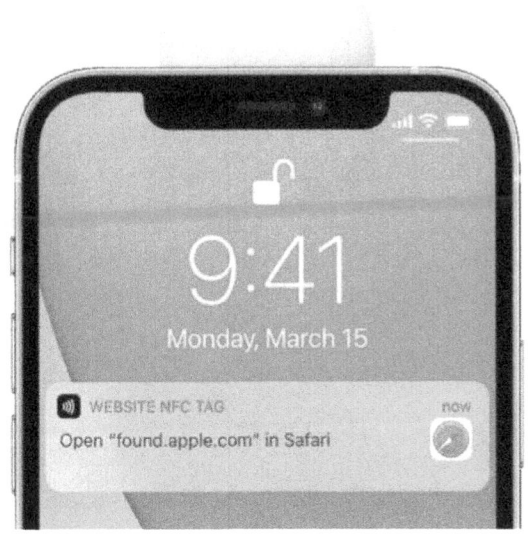

3 If the owner marks the AirTag as lost, a message with contact information may appear allowing you to contact the owner to let them know they have found their AirTagged item.

AirTags can only be used for tracking via iPhone or iPad with Find My app . Apple sells individual AirTags for $ 29, or four-packs for $ 99.

AIRTAG WATER RESISTANCE

Apple has made sure that the AirTag is durable by being IP67 rated, meaning AirTag is resistant to flight, water, and dust. If you throw the AirTag into the sink, into the pond, or stick in the rain, you don't have to worry about it being destroyed.

According to Apple

The AirTag has been tested in a controlled laboratory environment and is resistant to spills, water, and dust, IP67 rated according to IEC 60529 (maximum depth one meter, up to 30 minutes). Resistance to spills, water, and dust is not constant, and the resistance may decrease due to normal wear.

SHARING AIRTAG WITH FAMILY MEMBERS

Apple's new AirTag trackers have been approaching customers since Friday, and although the company has tried to outline ways to locate lost items, many users remain surprised and disappointed to learn that AirTag's location cannot be shared with other family members.

airtags

On its face, sharing AirTag's location through Apple Family Sharing is no problem, as some members of the Family Sharing group can use the Find My app to view other family members 'Apple devices, such as iPhones and iPads, Mac, AirPod, and Apple Watch.

Because of these family sharing privileges, many users have realized that an AirTag attached to an item that is regularly used by more than one person in the home (such as a key set) can be tracked by many family members in Find My.

Unfortunately, AirTags don't work like other apple devices in Find MY APP

CHAPTER FOUR

HOW TO HOW TO SET UP AIRTAGS

You can use AirTag to keep track of everyday objects, such as keys or a backpack. Learn how to set up AirTag on your iPhone, iPad, or iPod touch.

What you need

> ➢ iPhone, iPad, or iPod touch with iOS 14.5 or iPadOS 14.5 or later, and 2-factor authentication is turned on.
> ➢ My search.
> ➢ Bluetooth is turned on.
> ➢ Strong Wi-Fi or mobile connection.
> ➢ Location Services On Go to Settings> Privacy> Location Services.
> ➢ To use Precision Search and view your AirTag's most accurate location, turn on Location Search for My Search. Go to Settings> Privacy> Location Services, then scroll down and tap My Search.

Select the While using an application or
While using an application or modules check box.
Then turn on Exact Location.

If you have an Apple Managed ID, you can't set up AirTag.

SET UP YOUR AIRTAG

1. Make sure your machine is ready to set up.
2. If your AirTag is new, unpack the product and pull out the tab to activate the battery. AirTag will speak.
3. 3. Tap Connect while holding your AirTag next to your iPhone, iPad, or iPod touch. If you have multiple AirTags and see "Multiple AirTags Found," make sure there is only one AirTag at a time.
4. Select an item name from the list, or select a unique name to enter the AirTag name and select an emoticon. Then tap Continue.
5. To resume AirTag with your Apple ID, tap Continue again.
6. Tap Done.

You can now attach the AirTag to your item and view it in Find My App.

NOTE: You can also set up AirTag in Find My App. Tap the Items tab, then tap Add Item.

RENAME YOUR AIRTAG

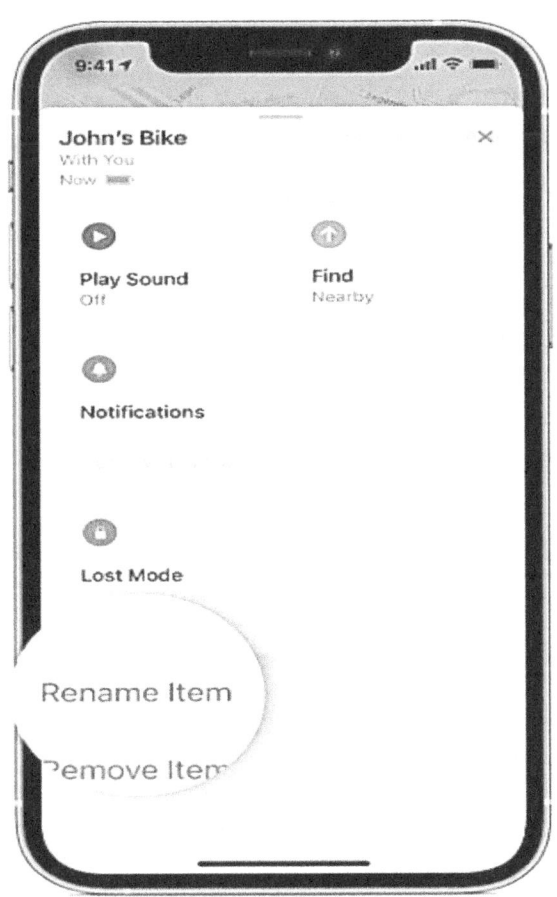

1. Open Find My, then tap the Items tab.
2. Tap the AirTag whose name or emoticon you want to change.

3. Scroll down and tap Name.
4. Select a name from the list or select a unique name.
5. Enter a special name for the AirTag and select an emoticon.
6. Tap Done.

IF YOU CANNOT SET UP THE AIRTAG

1. Make sure your machine is ready to set up.
2. If you need to set up multiple AirTags, make sure there is only one at a time.
3. Remove the AirTag's battery and replace it.
4. If the AirTag still does not connect to the device, reset the AirTag application.

Find out what to do if a message appears stating that the AirTag is connected to another Apple ID.

CHAPTER FIVE

CONNECTING AIRTAG FOR THE FIRST TIME

To connect the AirTag for the first time, the user must hold an iPhone, iPad, or iPad touch. If you're already close to your Apple device, tap Connect when it appears on the screen. The user can then either select a name from the list or create a unique name for the AirTag.

After selecting the name, tap Continue and register your AirTag with your Apple ID. Finally, tap Continue to complete the installation process.

If it is a brand new AirTag, the user must remove the packaging and the tab attached to the tracker. The tab turns off the battery and after removing it, the user hears an audible sound confirming that the AirTag is now working. Also, if you purchase more than one AirTag, you can only connect one at a time. In situations where more than one person is near the iPhone during the activation process, the user is likely to display a "Multiple AirTags Found" message. This message can be avoided by simply having only one AirTag near the iPhone at a time.

PREVENT UNWANTED TRACKING

AirTags are useful for tracking lost accessories. But Bluetooth detectors are also very capable of tracking people.

To avoid unwanted tracking, Apple allows users to disable AirTags on site. This can be done in a few simple steps.

First things first: Upgrade to iOS 14.5 now

When an unknown AirTag travels with you, a pop-up notification appears on your iPhone that says, "AirTag can be found with you."

To receive security notifications, you must first run iOS 14.5. The new software update is essential to access all of AirTags 'security features. Therefore, please do not delay updating to the latest software.

If you're unsure whether or not your smartphone is compatible with the latest update, here's a list of Apple items that do:

- ➤ iPhone 6S and later
- ➤ iPhone SE (1st and 2nd generation)
- ➤ iPod Touch (7th generation)
- ➤ 11-inch iPad Pro (1st and 2nd generation)
- ➤ iPad Pro 12.9-inch (1st, 2nd, 3rd, and 4th generation)
- ➤ iPad (5th, 6th, and 7th generation)
- ➤ iPad mini (4th and 5th generation)
- ➤ iPad Air (2nd and 3rd generation)

On your iPhone, iPad, or iPod Touch, navigate to Settings> General> Software Update and hit Download.

HOW DO I FIND MY AIRTAG ON MY IPHONE?

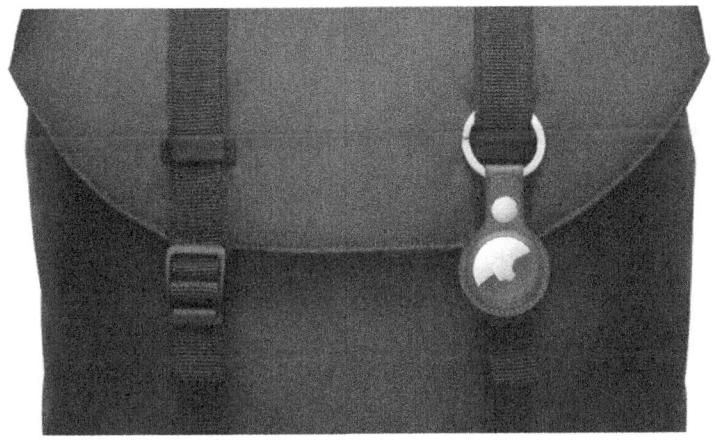

If you just set up a new AirTag, you need to know how to follow it to find the attached item when it runs out. If you're running iOS 14.5 / iPadOS 14.5 or later on your iPhone or iPad, you can use Find My App to find the missing AirTag associated with your Apple ID. Here's how.

VIEW THE LOCATION OF THE AIRTAG

In Find My, tap Items, then tap the item you want to find.

➢ If the object is found, it will appear on the map. The updated location and timestamp appear below the article name.

➢ If the item is not found, see where and when it was last. To be notified again, turn on Notification when you find an option in the

"Notifications" section.

INSTRUCTIONS ON HOW TO MAKE AN AIRTAG PLAY A SOUND

If the AirTag is nearby, you can get it to play sound so you can find it more easily.

1. In the Find My app, tap items.
2. Tap the AirTag you want to play.
3. Tap Play Sound.

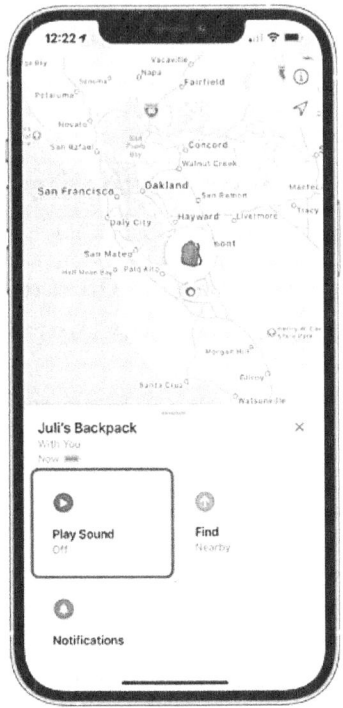
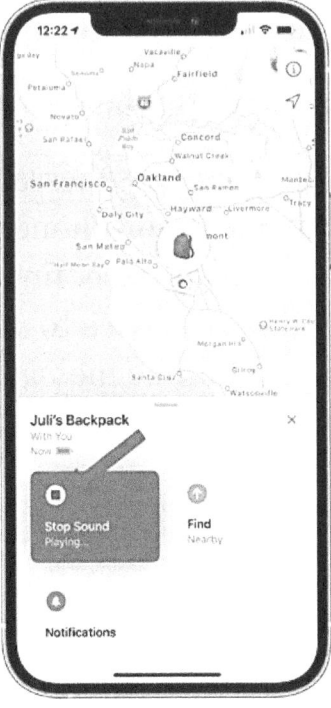

To stop playing the sound before it ends automatically, taps Stop sound.

You can also get a map route to the current location or last known location of the item, and if you have a supported iPhone and are near AirTag, you can find its exact location.

HOW TO MARK AIRTAG AS LOST

If you lose an AirTag (iOS 14.5 or later) or a third-party product (iOS 14.3 or later) registered in your Apple ID, you can use the Find My app to mark it as lost.

What happens if I mark an item as lost?

➢ You can add a message stating that the item is lost and enter your phone number.
➢ If someone else finds your item, you can use a supported device to view the Web site that contains the Lost Mode message.

TURN ON LOST MODE FOR AN ITEM

To mark an item as lost, you must turn on Lost mode.

1. Tap Items, then tap the lost item's name.
2. Under Lost Mode, tap Enable.
3. Follow the on-screen instructions to enter the available phone number. You may also be notified when an updated entry for an item appears in My Search.
4. Tap Active.

IN THE LOST MODE MESSAGE, CHANGE THE PHONE NUMBER

1. Tap Items, then tap the lost item's name.
2. Under Lost Mode, tap Enabled.
3. Edit the phone number, then tap Save.

TURN OFF LOST MODE FOR AN ITEM

If you find a lost item, turn off Lost mode.

1. Tap Items, then tap the item name.
2. Under Lost Mode, tap Enabled.
3. Tap Turn off lost mode.

CHAPTER SIX

HOW TO RETURN THE AIRTAG TO FACTORY SETTINGS FOR OTHERS TO USE

When you set up AirTag, it automatically associates with your Apple ID, which means it's associated with your "Apple ID" and no one else can use it unless you reset it.

Restoring can be as easy as removing the AirTag from your Apple ID by following these steps:

1. Open Find My app.
2. Tap the AirTag you want to remove by selecting its name from the list.
3. Drag up to view the full AirTag settings.
4. Touch "Remove Item". Remove the airbag

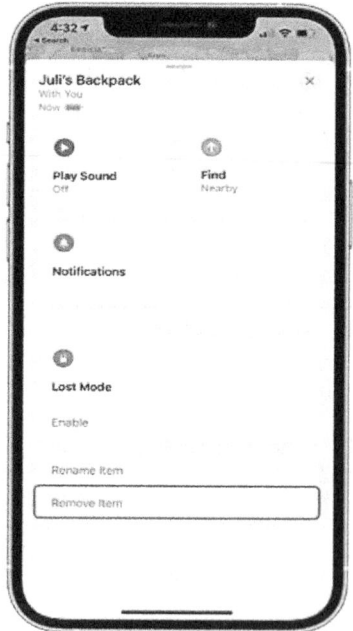 

5. Touch "Remove", then touch the "Remove" pop-up window again.

Once you have completed this process, AirTag will be de-owned and transferred to another person to set up and use with your account.

Unfortunately, if you are not within range of the AirTag Bluetooth when you remove it from your account, it will not register and you will need to perform a manual reset. If you receive an AirTag from someone else who says it is associated with your ID but has already removed it from your account, follow these steps to physically reset your AirTag:

1. Press down on the back of the AirTag stainless steel.
2. When you press, turn left until the cover stops rotating.

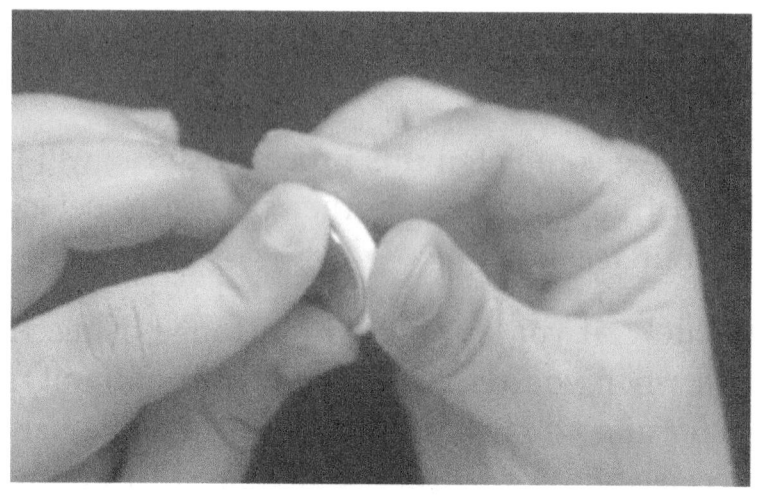

Airtag battery screw open

3. Pull out both halves of the AirTag.

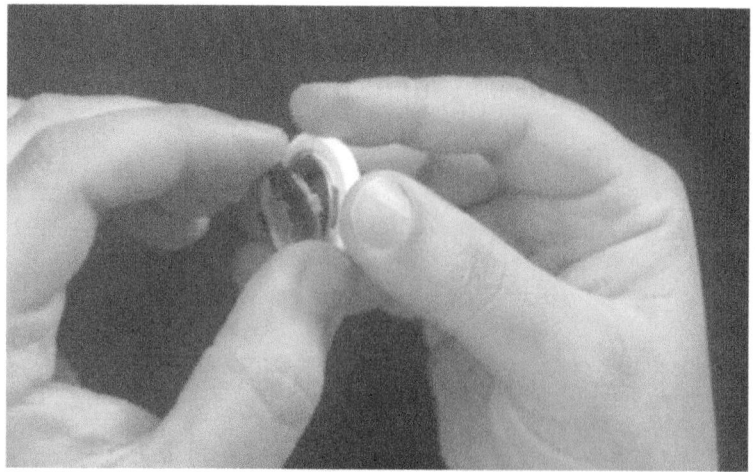

Separated Airtag element

4. Remove the battery.
5. Replace the battery.
6. Press the battery until it sounds.
7. As soon as the sound runs out, repeat this process four more times, remove and replace the battery, and then press the battery until you hear a sound.

Airtag element removed

8. You should hear a total of five beeps to make sure the AirTag is reset.
9. After completing this process, replace the AirTag cover, and then align the three tabs on the cover with the three openings on the AirTag.

10.   Press down on the cover until it sounds, and turn the cover to the right until it clicks into place.

To avoid having to go through this annoying physical recovery process, it's best to make sure the person receiving the AirTag is properly removed from your account while you're in the Bluetooth domain, as this is a much easier process for AirTag ownership delete the onward transfer to someone else

ABBREVIATIONS AIRTAG NFC

While AirTags is the most useful way to find things, Apple has decided to throw in NFC (near-field communication) compatibility there as well. With this, you can scan the AirTag with your iPhone or Apple Watch, bring it close, and then use Apple Shortcuts to launch a variety of actions.

The Apple Shortcuts app is pre-installed on your iPhone and iPad, but you can download it from the App Store if you've uninstalled it before.

If you don't already have an AirTag, you can buy one for $ 29 - or buy a four-pack for $ 99. If you already have an AIrTag, you can use your existing AirTags to do so and continue to use them as item tracking. Even when shortcuts are launched via NFC, AirTags continue to fulfill their primary purpose as trackers.

Therefore, you need to carefully think about what you want to start on AirTag and connect it to everything you keep track of. For example, if you have an AirTag in your bag, you might want to use it to start Do Not Disturb mode, start a workout, and convert your running playlist to Apple Music format.

AIRTAG PRIVACY AND SECURITY

We're revising today the period after which AirTag, separate from its owner, will speak when it is relocated, as part of our commitment to continue to strengthen AirTag's privacy and security," an Apple spokesman said. Resolution This time span can range from three days to anywhere between eight and twenty-four hours.

This may seem like a small change, but it is meant to handle that Apple hasn't done enough to prevent AirTags from being abused.

The Washington Post reported that the previous three-day window had made it "scary" for a potential stalker to follow the victim for days before receiving any warning that the AirTag had been secretly placed in its belongings.

To further alleviate privacy concerns, Apple is also designing an Android app to help users discover "an AirTag or Find My network-compatible accessory, separate from its owner, who may be traveling with a user."

Importantly, the app doesn't appear to be designed to provide Android users with full AirTags functionality, but it does give non-iPhone owners the ability to locate unwanted trackers. On the one hand, it still burdens a potential victim of theft to proactively download a new app and locate AirTag, which seems unrealistic. On the other hand, it shows that Apple is responding to privacy concerns and is open to improving the existing features of the anti-theft device.

Made in the USA
Middletown, DE
14 July 2023

35094203R00038